CELTIC M̶ ̶̶OGY

A Concise Guide to the Gods, Sagas and Beliefs

Copyright © 2016 by Hourly History.

Table of Contents

Introduction

Invocation to the Dagda

Hail Eochaid Ollathair, Father of All!
Hail Ruad Ro-fhessa, Lord of Perfect Knowledge!
Lord of the Oak Tree,
Phallus of the summer saplings,
Rough as tree bark is your wisdom,
Yet deep as sunken roots.
You who can call the seasons with your harp,
You are called upon by the common people
For your gift of fair weather.
You whose club is so great
That nine men are required to carry it
And even then it plows a great ditch;
Whose terrible end slays hundreds at a blow
And whose other end can restore them to life;
You stake your life on the fertility of the land
That others may survive the cold winters.
You who build great fortresses,
You know what it is to be the sole protection
Of those you love, and to go forth
In battle to save their lives.

—By Cianaodh Óg from Our Pantheon's Way

The land we call Ireland today boasts an ancient monument that is older than both the Sphinx and Stonehenge and served both as a place of worship as well as a royal burial chamber. Called Newgrange, this ancient building is located in County Neath, on the River Boyne. Newgrange is what archaeologists used to call a passage tomb. It is large; 85 meters in diameter and 13.5 meters high, covering nearly an acre. Newgrange is a sophisticated and intricately designed and decorated structure, and archaeologists are confident that it doubled as a place of ritual worship. At the Winter Solstice, the sun penetrates to the central inner chamber, which remains lit for about 17 minutes each year.

Newgrange was probably constructed by the first peoples who lived in Ireland. The earliest peoples are called the **Partholonians**, and they seem to have been wiped out by some dreadful disease, perhaps a plague, or destroyed by the tribe led by Nemed, said to be descended from the biblical Noah. The great **Nemedian** druid Mide is said to have been the first to light a fire in Ireland, at Uisnech. The traveling agrarians who washed up on those shores included Indo-Iranians, Scythians, Germanic and Slavic peoples, Grecians, Europeans, Central and South Asian traders, adventurers and warriors. In time, they also came from Austria, Bavaria, Switzerland, and the Balkans. Mostly, though, they were ferocious Gauls from France, Belgium, and the lowlands, with a generous sprinkling of Spanish wanderers.

The **Fir Bolg**, from Spain and Greece, originally served as slaves to the Nemedians, but soon gained ascendency over their masters; they divided Ireland into five parts and settled down to rule. They were then challenged by the people of the goddess Dana, who arrived from the north-west. These were known as **Tuatha dé Danann**, and they were to become the greatest aristocracy of Ireland. They fought the Fir Bolg at the First Battle of Moytura where their king, Nuada, lost a hand. After a four-day battle, the Tuatha dé Danann left the battlefield, and the Fir Bolg retained Connaught.

At about this time, there arose from the Tuatha dé Danann the powerful Irish god Eochaid Ollathair, who ruled in Ireland. He was the All-Father, God of Magic, God of Time, Protector of Crops, or the Dagda. He is one of the legendary figures said to be buried at Newgrange.

Chapter One

The Arrival of the Tuatha dé Danann

The story of the Tuatha dé Danann is told in the *Annals of the Four Masters* (*Annála na gCeithre Maístrí*) compiled by Franciscan monks. The Tuatha dé Danann, a mythical race of god-like beings with supernatural powers, came to Eire in the mists, or perhaps in a cloud, across the seas. They arrived with four magical possessions—treasures in fact—that played a significant part in Celtic mythology.

The first was the *Lia Fail*, the Stone of Destiny, upon which all Irish kings would be consecrated. The stone emitted a great roar when the rightful king stood upon it. The second was the *Claiomh Solais*, or Shinning Sword. This was an invincible sword of light, crafted by the poet and wizard Uiscias. It was always carried by King Nuada of the Silver Arm, and once drawn, it would always kill. The third treasure was Lugh's Spear. Its tip was fashioned of dark bronze, finely tapered and fastened to a rowan shaft by 30 rivets of gold. Much magic went into its making. The final possession was the Dagda's Cauldron. This large domestic container would never run out of food, and all who sat at it would be satisfied. It was made by a druid named Semias and imbued with such power that its abundant supply of food fed any number of warriors; additionally, it could heal any wound and even restore life.

This was more or less the time of the Bronze Age, and the following influx of people came mostly from Spain via Egypt and would go down in pre-Christian history as the **Milesians**. They came equipped with a new generation of iron weaponry, and the powerful Tuatha dé Danann were forced out of the mainstream. The resulting cultural clash of the natural powers of sun, moon, earth, and militarist bent of the Milesians, with the mystical, magical, and more intellectual beliefs of the Tuatha tribes, settled into the compromise that developed for many years. Broadly speaking, Ireland fell into two halves divided by the River Boyne.

Somewhere along this continuum of time are the beginnings of the Celtic Ireland we now recognize, although there are few original sources of its beginnings. A few sacred sites and some sculptural decorations on ancient monuments remain, but the insular literature that has survived is tainted by the fact that it was written so long after the event.

In the Book of Invasions, there is a story of the day the sons of Mil arrived on the Irish shoreline; the great poet Amhairghin set foot on land and declaimed:

I am a wind in the sea (for depth)
I am a sea-wave upon the land (for heaviness)
I am the sound of the sea (for fearsomeness)
I am a stag of seven combats (for strength)
I am a hawk upon a cliff (for agility)
I am a tear-drop of the sun (for purity)
I am fair (i.e. there is no plant fairer than I)
I am a boar for valour (for harshness)
I am a salmon in a pool (for swiftness)
I am a lake in a plain (for size)
I am the excellence of arts (for beauty)
I am a spear that wages battle with plunder.
I am a god who forms subjects for a ruler
Who explains the stones of the mountains?
Who invokes the ages of the moon?

Where lies the setting of the sun?
Who bears cattle from the house of Tethra?
Who are the cattle of Tethra who laugh?
What man, what god forms weapons?
Indeed, then;
I invoked a satirist...
a satirist of wind.

—With thanks to the Celtic Myth Podshow.
http://celticmythpodshow.com/Resources/Amergin.php

The history of Celtic mythology is held in the natural landscape, in the bloodlines of its people, in apparitions that manifest and then are gone as you glance their way. There is very little you can pin down, and there is much more than you can ever tell.

There were many, many great leaders and warriors during these times leading up to the birth of Christ. One Melisian king, who brought much order to the country, was Ollam Fodla, Doctor of Wisdom. He divided the country into Cantreds, appointing a chief, or Brugaid, over every territory, and a steward in every town. He established a school of learning and the *Feis of Tara*, which was a parliamentary gathering held once every three years and attended by chiefs, scholars, and citizens of the entire nation, to decide on governing principles for the country.

Another great ruler of Ulster at this time was Conor MacNessa, a king praised in many songs and stories. He was particularly fond of learning and poetry. He declared that great learning should be brought within the realm of the common man and that knowledge of the professions should not be held away from the masses as a way of exerting control over them. There is a curious legend attached to his death; he had a lead ball lodged in his brain as a result of an old battle with Cet MacMagach. He had survived seven years under the care of his doctor, Faith Liag, who had decided not to remove it because of its proximity to the brain. MacNessa, however, had to live a life of moderation, avoiding excessive emotional stress—not easy for an Irish king in those times. One mid-day there was the greatest upheaval in the heavens: the sun disappeared, and an impenetrable blackness fell on the earth. Thunder and lightning such as had never been seen before rent the air, and MacNessa summoned his wisest Druids and demanded an explanation.

They told him that "there had been in the East, a singular man, more noble of character, more lofty of mind, and more beautiful of soul, than the world had ever before known, or ever again would know—he was the noblest and most beautiful, most loving of men. And now the heavens and the earth were thrown into agony because on this day the tyrant Roman, jealous of his power over the people, had nailed him high upon a cross, and between two crucified thieves, had left the divine man to die a fearful death." Conor was so enraged by this that he lifted his great sword for the first time in years and set about bringing down a grove of trees nearby. This caused the lethal ball in his skull to explode, and Conor fell dead.

Chapter Two

Hibernia

Hibernia, the name for early Ireland, is historically the only land that escaped the tyranny of the growing Roman Empire. The Gauls had, in fact, sacked Rome as early as 392 BCE and then beat a hasty retreat. They had overrun Greece and attacked and looted Delphi in 279 BCE. But, the fierce Celtic warriors were finally to meet their match in Julius Caesar. Caesar became one of the sources we can use to continue the tale of Ireland from his records of the Gallic Wars in 58 to 51 BCE. He devotes a chapter in his extensive memoirs to document his fierce opponents, making many interesting observations of their way of life.

Caesar names five of their gods, using Roman gods as reference: Lugh or Lugus of the Long Arm, who he saw as the embodiment of the Roman god Mercury, the god of the arts, travellers, and commerce; Apollo, akin to Belenus, Oenghus, or Mabon, the god who drives away diseases; Mars and Jupiter, represented by Teutates, the Celtic god of war and heaven; Minerva, the Roman goddess of wisdom, was very similar to the popular Brigit, a goddess with many attributes, including handicrafts; finally, Caesar compared the Roman god Sucellos to the equivalent of the main Celtic god, the Dagda. Additionally, a very popular Celtic deity was adopted by Rome—Epona, the divine horse goddess, which came to be enthusiastically worshipped by the Roman cavalry.

It was about this time that the legendary tale *Táin Bó Cúalnge* took place, involving the lengthy war between Connacht and Ulster. It is known as the Iliad of Ireland and an appropriate place to end this timeline.

Creation Myths in Celtic Mythology

The white mare. Once upon a time, there were no gods or humans—only the land and the sea. Where the sea met the land, a white mare, Eiocha, made of sea-foam, was born. Nearby grew a sturdy oak tree, supporting a plant with white berries of "foam tears" from the sea. Eiocha ate these berries and grew heavy with child. She gave birth to the first god, Cernunnos. The birth was painful, and in her struggle, Eiocha ripped pieces of bark from the oak tree and threw them into the sea, thus creating the giants of the deep. Her offspring, Cernunnos, was very lonely and coupled with Eiocha to produce other gods: Maponus, Tauranus, Teutates, and the goddess Epona. Eiocha then returned to the sea and became Tethra, the goddess of the deep.

Work of the gods. Once upon a time, nothing existed except a few gods and a great oak tree. The gods created humans and the world. First, they fashioned a man and a woman from the wood of the oak tree. Cernunnos told the oak to grow forests, and he made several animals: deer, hounds, bears, ravens, hares, and snakes. Epona made a mare and a stallion. Teutates made bows, arrows, and a club. Tauranus also took wood from the oak and fashioned noisy thunderbolts and fire. Maponus fashioned an exquisite harp from oak wood; he played it with such mastery that the wind, the birds, and all the animals would gather to listen.

The giants, who lived in the sea, grew jealous and decided to overrun the land. Eiocha warned the gods, who took refuge in the oak trees and were then able to drive the giants back into the sea, where Tethra bound them to live forever. A few giants escaped; led by Fomhoire, they built a life on the outer perimeter of the world and plotted revenge on the land. Epona had rescued one man and one woman when the giants overran the land, and it is from them that the Irish people are born. New gods were born when the fiery pieces of heaven mixed with the tumultuous waters of the sea. The god Belenus, and Danu, his sister, were born from the initial fire, while Lir sprang from the contrasting elements of the settling waters, producing the powerful Manannan, the measured and wise Bran, and the most beautiful goddess Branwen. However, it was Danu who birthed the most important deities: the Dagda, Nuada of the Silver Hand, Diancecht the Wise, Goihbhio the Smith, Morrigan the Fearsome, and the Gentle Brigit.

The Primal Giant. Once upon a time, there was only ice. In the first winter, a powerful giant was created from the hoarfrost. An intense fire thawed the ice, and the giant's body became the world; his blood, the seas and oceans. His hair became the trees that formed the forests; his bones were the mountains and his skull, the sky. From this world, the gods arose and lived in the mountains and valleys of the underworld.

In 2002, a *seanchas* study was done at the Gerry Tobin Irish Language School in Babylon, New York, to reconstruct the lost Celtic creation myth. *Seanchas* is much more than genealogical research and includes the entire native tradition in history, law, social norms, and genealogy of a tribe. In this case, a team of researchers re-constructed the creation myth while examining the *Gabháil Cheasrach*, which is "The Taking of Ireland by Cessair" in the *Lebor Gabála Éren*, (Book of the Invasions), and comparing it to the Indo-European creation myths that still exist. It makes for interesting study, and you can find details online at http://www.irishtribes.com/articles/2012-11-lost-celtic-creation-myth-in-english.html

Chapter Three

The Main Gods of the Celtic Pantheon

There are over 300 names of Celtic deities, and many have several names. What follows is information about the most important gods.

The Dagda or Eochaid-Ollathair, the progenitor and All-Father. He is the leader of the Tuatha dé Danann and the god of life and death, the sun, prosperity, regeneration, banquets, and magic. He had immortal strength and an enormous appetite. He commanded a huge cauldron (called the Undry) with an endless supply of food, and he was always depicted with two pigs, one roasting, and one growing. He could kill many men with one blow of his excessively large club, but could also restore life using the other end. He played a magnificent and beloved harp with which he controlled the changing of the seasons and which would come to his hand when he called. Occasionally, he was represented as an almost comic figure in his joviality and in his slightly too short tunic that barely covered his shoulders and buttocks. Known as the Good God, his partners were the Morrigan and Boann, and he fathered Brigit and Aonghus.

The Morrigan, the Phantom Queen, was the goddess of war, fate, death, priests and witches, revenge, violence, and the patron of servicemen and women. The number three is sacred to her, and she is often in company with Fea, (Hate), Babd (Fury), and Macha (Battle). She brought the red-haired gene to the Irish. She does not take part in a battle, but, as a shapeshifter, she hovers overhead in the guise of a raven, a crow, and sometimes a vulture. She is Tuatha dé Danann royalty and helped defeat the Fir Bolg at the First Battle of Moytura and the Fomoriani at the Second Battle of Moytura.

When the great warrior Cú Chulainn was about to die, he attached himself to a stone to remain in an upright posture; it was only when a crow landed on his shoulder—a sign from the Morrigan—that his men accepted that he was dead.

Danu (Anu and Ana) is one of the very oldest earth goddesses and is the matriarch of the Tuatha dé Danann. She is also the mother and daughter of the Dagda and possibly another aspect of the Morrigan. Her consort is Bhe. Her name means knowledge, wisdom, teacher, and wealth, and she is known as the Flowing One—associated with many rivers in Europe, especially the Danube. She is the universal mother; with the coming of Christianity, she was demonized as a witch who ate children. She has a surprising following to this day, and there are many rituals which you can use to contact her using this invocation: "Lady Danu, mother of the gods and of the Tuatha dé Danann; great lady of the flowing waters, spirit of the rivers, mistress of the fertile lands, giver of abundant harvest—join me here. I ask you to be here."

Aonghus (Angus Og, Aengus, or Oengus of the Bruig) is the very complex god of love, youth, beauty, music, protection of lovers, dream work, and creativity. He played irresistible music on a silver harp. Four swans circled his head, and they are said to be the origin of the four X's one places at the end of a letter to represent four kisses. He owned a beautiful sword called *Moralltach*, the Great Fury, and a dun cow, both given to them by Manannan. He also had a magnificent horse.

Aonghus was the result of an affair between the Dagda and Boann, water goddess of the Boyne. To hide this encounter, the Dagda made the sun stand still for nine months, so Aonghus was conceived, grown and born on one day. He was brought up by Midir and was a fine, brave, beautiful young man, and a loyal friend—often speeding to help other gods. In the "Dream of Angus," it is told that he fell in love with a beautiful maiden he saw in a dream. After much searching, he found her chained with 150 others destined to be turned into swans on the feast of Samhain. Her name was Caer Ibormeith, and he was told he could marry her only if he could identify her after she had turned into a swan. Aonghus succeeded. Turning himself into a swan and, singing an enchanting song that put everybody to sleep for three days, they both flew away together.

Lugh, the Shining One or Lugh of the Long Hand is one of the most beloved of the gods. He is also known as Lug and Ildánach and sometimes, mistakenly, as Nuada of the Silver Arm. His grandfather, Balor of the Evil Eye, lived in fear of a myth that foretold his grandson would kill him. He, therefore, locked his only daughter, Ethlinn, in a crystal tower. Nevertheless, by way of magic means, Cian fathered Lugh with Ethlinn, and in a fury, Balor threw the infant into the roaring sea to drown. Lugh was saved and nurtured by the sea god Manannan Mac Lir, and he grew into fine manhood. He was handsome, youthful and energetic, and always remained young. He had an impressive list of gifts and talents being a wright, a warrior, a champion, a harpist, a sorcerer, a cup-bearer, a brazier, a poet, a musician, a gifted blacksmith, a scholar, and a physician.

Lugh offered all these arts and gifts when he applied to enter the ranks of the Tuatha dé Danann at Tara, where he presented himself thus: "Here there is Lugh Lonnannsclech son of Cian son of Dian-cecht, and of Ethne daughter of Balor. Fosterson, he, of Tallan daughter of Magmor king of

Spain and of Echaid the Rough, son of Duach." Despite this lineage, they would not let him enter, saying that they had among them at least one person who had such a particular skill as he presented. Lugh was also very inventive and smart, so he said: "Ask the king whether he has a single man who possesses all these arts, and if he has I will not enter Tara." Then the king ordered all the chess players to come forward, and when Lugh had won all the games, the king consulted Nuada, who said: "Let him into the garth, for never before has a man like him entered this fortress." Thus, Lugh the Shining One took his rightful place.

Lugh is always honored at the Festival of Lughnasadh in August, and he is the patron of Lyons. He also fulfilled the myth when he killed Balor at the Second Battle of Moytura (*Mag Tuireadh*) by smashing his evil eye right through the back of his skull with a brilliant sling shot. (The quotes are from: CELT: Corpus of Electronic Texts: a project of University College, Cork College Road, Cork, Ireland. http://www.ucc.ie/celt)

Diancecht is one of the more confusing and complex gods. Also known as Dian Cecht, Cainte, and Canta, he was a druid and healing magician of the Tuatha dé Danann. The name Diancecht means "strong plow," and it harks back to the importance of skilled craftsmen, even among the gods. Diancecht is remembered for his skill as a silversmith as well as his use of healing magic. He created a sacred and blessed well called the *Tobar Slaine*, the Well of Health, where all the Tuatha dé Danann who became ill or were injured in battle would be completely healed. The remains of this can be seen at the Heapstown Cairn in County Sligo.

This magic healing did not work in the case of a decapitation and one other instance; when Nuada, the leader of the Tuatha dé Danann, suffered a severe injury to his arm in a battle, he had to give up the throne, as a Celtic ruler could not continue to occupy the throne if he were maimed in any way. Although Diancecht fashioned him a spectacularly successful silver hand, Nuada was still forced to step aside; Bres, the leader of the Foramini, was appointed king in an attempt to heal the feud between these two major tribes. This brought out the worst side of Bres' disposition; his greed, avarice, and sly hypocrisy eventually resulted in the People of the Goddess virtually living as slaves—a position that could not be tolerated by the gods of the Tuatha dé Danann.

One of the signs of this state of affairs was the fact that Nuada's wrist festered where the silver hand joined his arm. Diancecht had several children, two of whom, Miach and Airmid, were also skilled healers, and Miach was able to restore Nuada's arm perfectly by retrieving the severed hand and uttering an incantation over it as follows: "Sinew to sinew, and nerve to nerve be joined." The hand healed, and Nuada led the battle to retrieve the throne successfully.

Diancecht, instead of rejoicing, was infuriated by his son's superior skill, and in a fit of jealous rage, took his son's life by deliberately wounding him in several increasingly severe attacks and ordering him to heal himself. This Miach did until his father struck him on the head, through the brain, to the neck—a wound even he could not heal. Myth has it that 365 different healing herbs grew on Miach's grave. Airmid carefully separated all the medicinal herbs and plants according to their healing properties, but her distraught father destroyed the methodically tabled order, thus causing us forever to lose our ability to know which plant to use for which ill. Many mythologies present stories of familial conflict, especially between father and son, but this instance of jealousy between two protagonists concerning the gift of healing is unusual.

Arawn, God of the Otherworld, the Underworld, or the Dead, is also known as Arawyn or Arawen. Remember that in Celtic mythology, the Underworld is not a dark place but a pleasant, light place where one lives happily if one has led a good life on earth. Arawn is also a god of war, terror, revenge, and spirit contact. His best-loved pastime is hunting through the sky in autumn, winter, and early spring with his large pack of white, red-eared dogs, in search of stags and deceased human souls, whom he guides to the Otherworld. On the hunt, he is often accompanied by a frightening hag called Matilda of the Night.

Genealogy of Brigit

The genealogy of the holy maiden Brigit,
Radiant arrow of flame, noble foster-mother of gods,
Brigit the daughter of the Dagda,
Dagda the Good God, the son of Ethlinn,
Ethlinn the daughter of Balor,
Balor the king of the Fomoire.

Every day and every night
That I say the genealogy of Brigit,
I shall not be killed, I shall not be injured,
I shall not be enchanted, I shall not be cursed,
Neither shall my power leave me.

No earth, no sod, no turf shall cover me,
No fire, no sun, no moon shall burn me,
No water, no lake, no sea shall drown me,
No air, no wind, no vapour shall sicken me,
No glamour out of Faery shall o'ertake me,
And I under the protection of the holy maiden,
My gentle foster-mother, my beloved Brigit.

—Ancient songs collected by Alexander Carmichael in *Carmina Gadelica*.

Brigit, the Exalted One. Also known as Bridgit, Brigindo, Bride, and Mistress of the Mantle, she is a goddess of fire, the forge, light and the sun, wells and springs, healing, childbirth, poetry, smithcraft, and martial arts. She was born as the sun rose, and wherever she walked, small flowers and shamrocks would appear. She grew up on the milk from a sacred white cow that lived in the Otherworld. She was so beloved by the Celtic people that she had to be assimilated to Christianity as St. Bridget. Her father was the Dagda; her mother, the Morrigan. She was married to Bres, in an effort to heal a rift that had opened between the Irish tribes, but this strategy was a failure.

Brigit had three sons: Ruadan (Brian), Luchar, and Uar, all famous warriors. When Ruadan was killed in battle, her grief was overwhelming, and her lamentations were heard around the universe—this is said to be the origin of the Irish custom of keening at a death. She had threefold power from fire: the Fire of Inspiration, manifesting in poetry; the Fire of the Hearth, manifesting in midwifery and healing; and the Fire of the Forge, manifesting in exquisite smithcraft and all the martial arts. At her shrine in Kildare, a perpetual flame was tended by the women who studied with her, and it burned brightly for over one thousand years. It was extinguished during the Reformation by King Henry VIII as Bridget's persona was slowly Christianized.

You can still visit her sacred well at Kildare. Tradition has it that you dip a little piece of cloth called a *clootie* into the water, and then wipe it over a wound that needs healing. You then tie the *clootie* to the rag tree nearby, usually an ash or whitethorn tree, as an offering to the spirit of the well and, as the cloth disintegrates, so your wound or illness would be healed. There are such wells dedicated to the goddess Brigit all over Ireland, Scotland, and Britain.

Vigil at the Well

A rock ledge. A dark pool.
Pale dawn and cold rain.
And a woman alone
holding three coins.

She circles the well
three times in the rain.
She offers the coins
to a great ancient tree
then bends to the pool.

A glimmer of silver.
Dawn striking the pool?
A fish in its depths?
The pool stills again.
The sky blazes red.
The woman gets up.
Nothing seems changed.

But the next day a wind
blows warm from the sea.

—Patricia Monaghan

Boann, Goddess of the River Boyne. Also known as Boannan and Boyne. She also has powers of healing, fertility, and water magic. Her husband was Nechtan, the god of water and the guardian of the Sidhe Nechtan, the

Well of Segais, the fountainhead of knowledge and wisdom. The well was surrounded by nine hazel trees of wisdom, and the nuts used to fall into the well and feed the speckled salmon who lived there. This is the origin of the myth that salmon are great guardians of knowledge.

No one except Nechtan and his cupbearers was allowed to approach the well. Boann was curious, and whether it was a desire for more power, a thirst for wisdom, or perhaps seeking cleansing from conceiving her son, Aonghus, by the Dagda, she approached the well one day while she was walking her dog, Dabilla. She circled it three times widdershins, or anticlockwise, challenging the water and chanting an incantation. The waters of the well rose up and swept them both away as it flooded the land and forged a pathway to the sea. This became the River Boyne. In some versions of the myth, the waters divided into five streams, each representing one of our senses; sight, taste, smell, touch, and hearing. Manannan, the great god of the sea, said: "The fountain which thou sawest, with the five streams out of it, is the Fountain of Knowledge, and the streams are the five senses through which knowledge is obtained. And no one will have knowledge who drinketh not a draught out of the fountain itself and out of the streams."

Maeve (Medb) is an exceptionally interesting deity, and also a historical figure as the Queen of Connaught. Her name means either "intoxicated" or "intoxicating woman," and she was both, with her long, golden hair and her fiery temperament. She was incredibly strong, a brilliant and inspiring warrior, a horsewoman par excellence, a fine hunter, and a charismatic—or perhaps demented—leader, intensely competitive and fiercely persistent. She represented the height of feminine power and rewarded her most outstanding soldiers with delightful sexual favors. The troops all competed for "Maeve's willing thighs," and she had no problems in dispensing this reward, as she boasted that she required 32 men a night to satisfy her sexual needs. However, her favorite lover was Fergus Roich of the Red Branch.

An argument with her consort, the High King Ailill, not about infidelity as you might imagine but more about inequality, would bring about one of the best-known sagas of Celtic mythology in the *Táin Bó Cúaligne*, called the "Brown Bull of Cooley." You can visit *Misgaun Maeve*, her burial mound in Knocknarea in Count Sligo. Sadly, she too was tamed by the fierce Christianity which took root in Ireland with the arrival of St. Patrick in 432 CE. You will be surprised to find her, unrecognizable, in the guise of Titania, the Fairy Queen in Shakespeare's *A Midsummer Night's Dream* or as Queen Mab in his *Romeo and Juliet*.

Queen Mab

Her chariot is an empty hazelnut,
Made by the joiner squirrel or old grub,
Time out o' mind the fairies' coachmakers.
And in this state she gallops night by night
Through lovers' brains, and then they dream of love;
O'er courtiers' knees, that dream on curtsies straight;
O'er lawyers' fingers, who straight dream on fees;
O'er ladies' lips, who straight on kisses dream,
Which oft the angry Mab with blisters plagues,
Because their breaths with sweetmeats tainted are.

—Extract from Mercutio's speech in *Romeo and Juliet* by Shakespeare.

Her gravitas is perhaps better served in Percy Bysshe Shelley's great philosophical poem:

Queen Mab

I am the Fairy MAB: to me 'tis given
The wonders of the human world to keep;
The secrets of the immeasurable past,
In the unfailing consciences of men,
Those stern, unflattering chroniclers, I find;
The future, from the causes which arise
In each event, I gather; not the sting
Which retributive memory implants
In the hard bosom of the selfish man,
Nor that ecstatic and exulting throb
Which virtue's votary feels when he sums up
The thoughts and actions of a well-spent day,
Are unforeseen, unregistered by me;
And it is yet permitted me to rend
The veil of mortal frailty, that the spirit,
Clothed in its changeless purity, may know
How soonest to accomplish the great end
For which it hath its being, and may taste
That peace which in the end all life will share.
This is the meed of virtue; happy Soul,
Ascend the car with me!

—By Percy Bysshe Shelly from *Queen Mab*

Goibniu, the Swordsmith of the Gods, was a vital link in the power of the people of the Tuatha dé Danann. He was the god of blacksmiths and metal craft, and he made all the major weaponry for the warriors of the goddess Dana. He worked with two other gods, some say his brothers, Luchtain the carpenter and Creidhnc the bronze wright, and they were known as the *Tri Dée Dána*. In the great battles between the Tuatha and the Fomorians, the latter was always frustrated by the fact that they would kill the same soldiers, carrying brand new weapons, day after day. In frustration, they sent a spy to the Tuatha camp to discover the secret of this magic. The spy reported that "he saw how Goibniu forged lance-heads with three blows of his hammer, while Luchtainé cut shafts for them with three blows of his axe, and Credné fixed the two parts together so adroitly that his bronze nails needed no hammering in."

It was simple, really; every weapon forged by Goibniu "always found its mark and never failed to kill" and the bodies of the dead and wounded warriors were all dipped in the magic *Tobar Slaine*, the Well of Health, and were fully restored. There may have been another factor: there are many myths about Goibniu and several mention that he also had a reputation for a potent brew—something between mead and beer—that bestowed eternal youth and sometimes even eternal life on those who drank it. Suitable quantities of this drink were, of course, distributed before major battles.

Chapter Four

Celtic Life and Rituals

Broadly speaking, the Celtic expansion reached its height around 225 BCE, and the mythology we are exploring dominated the cultural milieu for people's lives right down through the Middle Ages. It was an agrarian culture for the most part, but it was not without wealth; archaeological investigations have come across over 400 Celtic gold mine sites in France alone.

They had an oral tradition, and bards would recite the great sagas of the people at the three yearly gathering at the *Feis of Tara*, where the governing rules were reviewed, major disputes were resolved, and new laws and regulations would be promulgated. It is said that five great roads radiated across the country from Tara Hill to the five regions, each ruled by a king or a *Ri Tuath*. These are Ulster in the north, Connaught in the west, Munster in the south, Leinster in the east, and Mide (Meath) at its center. Returning to Julius Caesar's description of the Celtic people, he characterized them as mysterious and superstitious. One description of the Irish people states they were a "conglomeration of tribes with remarkable staying power."

Regarding social structure, the majority of the farmers were *Feines* or freemen. People certainly honored their ancestors and were close to the gods they worshipped. They were tightly organized around kinship groups, known as clans. The largest clans would be headed by a chief or *Taoiseach*; smaller clans would have a chieftain. The leaders were of the *Flaith* or noble class. One could even be the "chieftain of one cow" a *Bo-Aire*, but the duty of the designated head to protect the clan and its property was sacred under Breton Law until well into the seventeenth century.

There was also a respected class of craftsmen and artisans. The prestigious and well-loved bards came next, and they were the keepers of the peoples' history, which they recited in the traditional stories and songs. The druids were the religious leaders and the link to the spiritual realm; they were also the teachers, the philosophers, the astronomers, the healers, the politicians, and the judges. Essentially, a senior druid would have a long apprenticeship behind him—typically 20 years—and he often wielded as much power as a minor king. The overall ruler was known as the *Ri Cóicid*.

The Celtic people seldom built temples—they had no need. The sanctity of nature was an inescapable part of their worship, and the land itself was a permanent temple. Sacred places were often located near a water source, especially a well, spring, or a lake. A grove of trees would come to surround hallowed ground. Sacred bogs have revealed human burial sites containing objects like statues, decorations, and the remnants of food and necessities for the journal to the Otherworld.

The bog burial sites also suggest that the Celts may well have performed human sacrifices at one time, as the evidence of several bodies found suggests violent death as a result of several causes—none of which natural. Sites were found in Gaul, Britain, and Ireland, the most famous being the Lindow Man found in Cheshire in 1984. Carbon dating put his death between 2 BCE and 119 CE, and a spokesperson from the British Museum has said, "Conserved for nearly 2,000 years by the acidic, anaerobic conditions, it was possible to make out his facial features, a distinctive furrowed brow with close-cropped hair and beard . . . For the first time, it was possible to see the face of a person from Britain's prehistoric past." There is no evidence that the Lindow Man, about 25 years old, was ill in any way, but he met the requirements for a ritual death which was that the victim must die as a result of three reasons at the same time: he had received a lethal blow to the head, he had been strangled with a garrote, and then thrown into a pool, face downward and unconscious, resulting in drowning. If it was a ritual death, what was the reason? To protect his clan from intruders? To ensure a good harvest? To bring a safe winter?

Celtic life and religious observation were tied to the farming cycle and, in a truly Irish way, it begins in winter with the observation of **Samhain**, around October 31 and November 1. At this time, the living were thought to be very close to those in the Otherworld—spirits could warm themselves at a communal hearth, and bards could sing their way across the threshold; festivals could be a little wild. The tribe's druids would use this time, usually at the darkest time of the night, to make contact and seek guidance from their ancestors. The chant would be "Cast away. Oh man and woman whatever impedes the appearance of light in your life." It was a time of bonfires, bringing in the cattle, and settling in for winter. Even the warrior elite put up their weapons and remembered their dead.

Then, in early spring, as the lambing time arrived and the ewes came into milk, the goddess Brigit would come into her own: there would be festivals of lighting fires and the blessing of water sources. This was the time of **Imbolc**, around February 1. A sheaf of new oats would be dressed in female clothes and placed in a "Bride's Bed" in honor of Brigit. It was a gentle time, and the druid festivals would include honoring the Mother Goddess with eight candles placed in a circle in a decorated vessel of spring water.

Beltane is the next seasonal festivity and is the origin of May Day. It is associated with Belenus, one of the sun gods; a purification ritual would implore the sun to release itself from its wintery death. It was also the start of the fighting season. It leads swiftly to the summer solstice on June 21 or 22 in the Northern Hemisphere and *Alban Heruin*, an important festival for druids. A vigil is held throughout the night, sitting around the solstice fire, followed by a Dawning Ceremony as the sun rises. This is a powerful time for the casting of spells. At noon a further ceremony is held; special herbs would be mixed with the burnt ashes from the bonfires and scattered over cattle herds and the land to ensure abundant yields. Twin bonfires would be lit, and all the clan's cattle would be passed between the two light sources, followed by those who would be hoping for a child in the coming year. It was customary to decorate special trees, like oaks, with ribbons. It was also a good time for personal renewal. If you are so minded, find a peaceful, natural place where you can relax and enjoy a communication with nature. When you are at ease, recite this version of Amhairghin's dedication when he first landed on Irish soil thousands of years ago:

I am the wind across a deep, wide lake.
I am the wave over the endless sea.
I am the stag of seven tines, racing through the woods
I am the eagle in the aerie, flying above the rocks
I am a flash of light from the sun above, bringing heat to
those below
I am the blooming plants, bringing sustenance and beauty
I am a wild boar, powerful and strong
I am the salmon in the water, swimming endlessly
upstream
I am the hill where poets stroll for inspiration

I am the head of the spear the draws blood in battle
I am the god that puts fire in the head and honor in the heart.

—With thanks to Patti Wigington.
http://paganwiccan.about.com/od/dreamsandmeditation/ss/Nature_Med.htm#step1

Lughnasadh is the final festival of the year and is sacred to the very popular deity Lugh. It usually lasted about two weeks and involved competitions associated with physical skills, particularly horses. Marriages were celebrated, and those joinings of the previous year that had been less than successful would be annulled after a suitable trial period. It fell around July 31, which also marks the start of harvesting for farmers. The fruits of the harvest were used for celebratory feasting; some grain would be set aside for the next planting season and the rest was stored away to feed the tribe during the winter.

Lughnasadh is a time to celebrate the warmth of summer, bearing in mind the coming of winter. In many areas, a flaming wheel was set rolling down the hillside, or a ceremonial wheel would be passed around a circle by the chief druid to bring to mind the turning of the year.

Chapter Five

Sources of Celtic Mythology

Some linguists call Gaelic, the native language of Ireland, the "Chosen Language" and claim that it was spoken in the Garden of Eden—that it came with Jacob's tribe to Egypt, then Carthage and via Galicia in Spain, to Ireland. The more conventional linguists will say the roots are Indo-European, and the reason why it is so incredibly rich is that it, like the people, has developed from 72 different languages. However it happened, Gaelic has been the spoken and written language of Ireland for thousands of years and was well established by 600 BCE. The oldest ancient Irish inscriptions we have are on stones that date from the fifth and sixth centuries. It is also spoken in Scotland, and today it is still the vernacular in Ireland, Scotland, Wales, the Isle of Man, Cornwell, and Brittany.

Language and poetry played an important part of life in ancient Ireland, and you will have noticed that most of the deities will have a strong connection to poetry in their powers and responsibilities. Ogmios, or Ogma, was the Celtic god of oratory, and he was depicted with beautiful chains of gold and amber attaching him, sometimes from his tongue to the ears.

There is a large body of written sources for Celtic mythology. Unfortunately, these written records were created as Christianity grew in the land, and many stories were sanitized; subtle (and not-so-subtle) adjustments were made to promote a very different culture. Some historians point out that Celtic mythology perhaps got off more lightly from this kind of censorship than other traditions, as most of the manuscripts were created by Irish monks, who would perhaps have been more intent on preserving Irish culture than saving souls.

The earliest writings were all destroyed by the marauding Vikings, and the records we are still able to consult were written in about the twelfth century. The earliest is known as the *Lebohr na h Uidhre* manuscript, or the *Book of the Dun Cow* (1130). A second manuscript survives from 1150 called *Lebohr Laigneck* or the *Book of Leinster*. A fourteenth-century manuscript called *Lebhar Buidhe Leácain* or the *Yellow Book of the Lecan*, presently held at Trinity College, is a miscellany of pieces in prose and verse. A later manuscript is the *Book of the Dean of Lismore* which contains poetry compiled by James MacGregor, circa 1480-1551, and is held at the National Library of Scotland. Another wonderful source is the *Lebor Gábala Érenn* (the Book of Invasions or the Book of the Taking of Ireland), which gives a history of the Irish people; last but not least, the text contains various versions of the first and second Battles of Mag Tuired or Battles of Moytura, which was fought by the Tuatha dé Danann, firstly against the Fir Bolg and then to escape the oppression of the Fomorians. The originals of these manuscripts are also held at the National Library of Scotland.

Great Celtic Sagas and Heroes

The great sagas and heroes of Ireland are captured in four cycles, all based on the literary sources above. The first is the **Mythological Cycle**, which is mostly taken up with the Tuatha dé Danann and the creation of Ireland itself. One such story, told below, is the saga of the Dagda's harp.

The Dagda's harp was one of his most treasured possessions. It was fashioned of noble oak, beautifully decorated and embellished with a doubled headed fish with jeweled eyes. He used it for many purposes; for instance, he played it to cause one season to follow another in proper order. He played it to instill hope and bravery in his men as they went into battle, and he played it at the end of a battle to soothe the weary warriors, assuage their grief at fallen comrades, and to mend their wounds. When the Fomorians were preparing to fight the Tuatha dé Danann in the second Battle of Moytura, they decided to steal the harp to distract their enemies in their war preparations.

They succeeded in both objectives; the Dagda was furious, and after the battle, which the Tuatha won notwithstanding, he, alongside his son Aonghus and Lugh of the Long Arm, set out to fetch it home. They tracked the defeated Fomorians down to the castle where they were gloating over the magnificent harp they had hung on the wall as their consolation prize for losing the battle. The Dagda sang out his magic chant to call the harp to him as follows:

"Come Daurdabla, apple-sweet murmurer
Come, Coir-cethair-chuir, four-angled frame of harmony,
Come summer, come winter,
Out of the mouths of harps and bags and pipes!"

The harp immediately swept off the wall and flew to the Dagda's hand, striking nine men dead as it traveled through the air. Hundreds of warriors awoke and grasped their weapons, turning on the three men. The Dagda struck the strings with his hands, and he played the Three Noble Strains of Ireland. First, he played the *Geantraí*, the strain of merriment, laughter and drunken foolery, and the Fomorians began to laugh out loud and toast one another as they danced; their weapons fell from their hands. They soon recovered and picked up their weapons to advance again upon the three. The Dagda then called forth the strain of *Goltraí*; the Fomorians began to weep in grief for the fallen, and again their weapons slid from their hands as their tears flowed and men hid their faces. Finally, the Dagda brought forth the strain of *Suantraí*; the warriors struggled, but slowly started falling asleep, dropping their weapons once more. The Dagda, his son, and Lugh left them sleeping there, and they made away with the harp, which was never stolen again.

The second cycle is the **Ulster Cycle**, which brings together many stories of the cult of great warriors and splendid battles. The central story is the *Táin Bó Cúailnge*, or the Cattle Raid of Cooley, and the story of the magnificent Celtic warrior Cú Chulainn. The following story is how this exceptional youth acquired his name.

Conchobar, king of Ulster, was going with a small retinue to feast at the house of the well-renowned weaponsmith Cullan. On the way, he stopped at the boy's camp to watch the young men at their games. He was much struck by the boy Setanta, who excelled at all the games, particularly the sport of hurling. This old game is played with a ball about four inches in diameter and a hurley, a three-foot-long stick made of ash with a flattened and curved lower end. The game takes great strength and skill to play. The king invited Setanta to come along to the feast, and it was arranged that Setanta would follow when his training had finished by tracking the chariot tracks of the king's party.

When all his guests had settled down to the feast, Cullan inquired of the king whether he could set free the dog he had trained to guard his property. He explained that, as a tradesman who lived from his craft, he had very little land, and he did not retain warriors to keep him safe. Now this hound was no ordinary dog; he was the size of a pony, had the strength of over a hundred men, and had been trained by Cullan to attack and kill unless otherwise directed by his master. He was set free, and after doing a round of the property, the great dog settled down at the front door, his great head resting on his paws, but his red eyes alert and staring, unblinking, into the night.

Setanta, meanwhile, was following the king's trail swiftly. He passed the time by hurling a ball ahead of him and then racing to catch the ball before it fell to earth. He moved quickly, but he was also highly distracted; when he got to the house, the great hound let out a ferocious howl and headed straight for him. The only weapon Setanta had about him was the flimsy hurling stick and ball. Instinctively, he hurled with all his might—the ball went straight into the great dog's mouth and caused him to start choking. Setanta grabbed the dog by its hind legs and swung it around with all his might, dashing its brains out on a rock.

The guests came rushing out and rejoiced greatly that the boy had survived the encounter. Cullan, too, was relieved, but was also devastated by the death of his faithful servant; he wept for the hound that had protected him for so long. How was he to safeguard his household now? Setanta felt terrible when he heard the story, and he asked Cullan if he knew of a pup sired by his dog anywhere in Ireland. Cullan said he could get one, but it would take a long time to train him—how would he protect himself in the meantime? Setanta said he should acquire the pup, and for as long as it took Cullan to train him, Setanta would come and guard the household every night.

The chief druid, Cathbad, was among the guests. He said that henceforth Setanta would be called Cú Chulainn, i.e., "Cullan's hound," and he prophesied that one day that name would be renowned throughout the world. Cathbad also put a *geis*, or a prohibition or taboo of a kind, on Setanta, not to ever eat the flesh of a dog. Setanta accepted the change and was henceforth known as Cú Chulainn. For an entire year, he returned to the place every evening, made a circuit around the house holding, and settled down, like a dog, at the door—one eye open to protect Cullan's property from whatever threats might arise.

There are many sagas about Cú Chulainn and his colorful life. One of the most entertaining is how it came that he could claim the Champion's Portion. It is very long and complicated, as well as thought-provoking and enjoyable. You can read it at http://bardmythologies.com/ulster-cycle/

The third cycle is called the **Fenian Cycle** and deals with sagas involving the warriors and the lore of the Fianna—a roving, nomadic, almost outlaw band, whose main occupations were hunting and undertaking wondrous quests that, of course, usually involved fighting. Their mottoes were: "Strength of limb, purity of heart, and actions to match our words." Led by Finn Mac Cumhaill, the Fianna had strenuous physical and mental requirements for recruits who wished to join, including leaping, running, agility, stamina, and swordsmanship, as well as the ability to recite a formidable collection of sagas, tales, and poetry by heart.

The Fianna were respected where ever they went and would settle each winter with a different nobleman and earn their keep by protecting him. Apart from magnificent fighters, the Fianna had wise druids as well as gifted bards and storytellers in their band; they also possessed a particular treasure, Cumhaill's Oxter Bag. The bag was made of stork skin, and whatever it was that Cumhaill needed, he would only have to put his hand in the bag, and it would be his. Below is a story of the Fianna, known as "The Hostel of the Quicken Trees."

Once upon a time, the Fianna were called upon to beat back the invading army of the king of Lochlann and his sons. Generous in victory, Finn Mac Cumhaill spared the king's youngest son, Miadach, and brought him up with love as one of his fosterlings, settling him with some lands of his own as he reached adulthood.

One day the Fianna were out on a hunt after a giant boar. Finn and a few companions become separated from the main group. They came across Miadach, and after friendly greetings, Miadach invited them for a drink at the nearby Hostel of the Quicken Trees. The always grumpy Conan Maol Mac Morna was suspicious of this invitation, but Finn reprimanded him. Finn asked his son Oisín and three young warriors to wait with Diarmuid O'Duibhne and Caoilte Mac Ronán for the rest of the hunt while he, Conan Maol, and his brother Goll went to have a drink at the hostel.

It was a beautiful hostel, set in a grove of quicken trees and surprisingly luxurious with rich furnishings, a fire giving forth sweet smells, and colorful coverings on the floor. It took a few minutes for the Fianna to take all this in and to realize that Miadach was nowhere to be seen.

"Goll spoke up. 'Finn. Wasn't there a window there just a moment ago?' Finn agreed that there was. 'Then why is it only bare planks that I see now?' said Conan Maol, 'And

weren't there rich tapestries on those walls a moment ago?
And they bare now? And wasn't there a fire in that grate,
that's cold now? And furthermore, weren't we sitting on
grand fine couches a moment ago, when there's bare dirt
under us now!?' In fact, all the loveliness on the hostel had
vanished, and now it was a mean, bare hut, with no
windows and only one door, and a dirt floor under them."

Realizing something was amiss, the men tried to leap up and found that they were all stuck fast to the cold earth floor. At this point, Finn put his thumb between his teeth—the thumb he had burnt on the Salmon of Knowledge—and all was revealed to him. Miadach had brought the army of the king of Torrents across the seas, and they were on the way to destroy them. The spell had been cast upon them by this king, and only his blood could wash it away.

The three men then sounded the *Dord Fiann*, the war-cry of the Fianna. This brought two warriors, Fiachna and Innsa, from the waiting party on the run. When they heard the story, they set out to find the invading army. They made their stand at the bottom of the hill, at a ford that was the only possible approach to the hostel. Meanwhile, Oisín and Caoilte, the fastest runners, went off to gather the rest of the Fianna. All that night, Fiachna and Innsa fought off wave after wave of the enemy, holding the ford, while Finn and his two greatest warriors lay helpless, stuck to the floor. Both Fiachna and Innsa eventually died of their injuries, but they held the ford until the rest of the smaller hunting party came to their aid.

Diarmuid and Fodla hunted down the king of Torrents' three sons and cut off their heads. Diarmuid rushed the heads, streaming with blood, back to the hostel, leaving Fodla to hold the line once more. Diarmuid first went to Finn and set him free by bathing him in blood. Then he did the same with Goll Mac Morna, coming to Conan Maol last. He got Conan's arms and legs free, but his back still stuck firmly—by now, the blood had run out. Conan had always felt that Diarmuid was far too good looking to be a proper warrior; in his irritation, he yelled at Diarmuid: "You wouldn't leave me till last if I was a pretty woman, you useless preener!" With his arms and legs waving in the air and his back still firmly stuck down, Conan looked for all the world like a beetle. Finn and Goll, still weakened by the enchantment, managed to help Diarmuid to pull Conan to his feet, but all the skin ripped off his back; he was bleeding dreadfully. Finn sent Diarmuid back to the ford where warriors had arrived to reinforce what was left of the first invaders.

Finn's strength was returning, so he killed a black sheep that was grazing in a field nearby and covered Conan's back with the sheep's skin. This stuck firmly in place, probably as a result of the leftover adhesion spell, and they all set off to join the rest of the Fianna, who had arrived at the ford. Once the Fianna were there in force, the invaders were driven back with very few survivors. Every spring after that, Conan Maol's back had to be shorn of its wool.

The final cycle is known as the **King's Cycle** or the **Historical Cycle**. These tales are about the various fortunes of the Celtic kings. The well-being of the realm was directly linked to the quality of the king. Most of the kings were semi-historical figures with god-like power and influence. Kings and exceptional warriors were hugely powerful, but quite often also helpless in the face of a supernatural restriction called a *geis* placed on them, usually by a senior druid (*geasa* in the plural). To break a *geis* would immediately break a sacred bond between a leader and his people, so it was never done. It is quite a difficult concept, and the nearest one can get to explaining it nowadays is that it is a taboo. One Celtic historian explained a *geis* as "a signpost of destiny." For more on the King's Cycle see http://bardmythologies.com/king-cycle/ An exceptional online source for other mythological stories is http://emeraldisle.ie/map

Chapter Six

The Effect of Christianity and Celtic Superstitions

The "Chronicle of Prosper of Aquitaine," a historical record of the history of Christianity in Ireland, had the following entry for the year 431 CE: "Palladius was ordained by Pope Celestine and sent to the Irish believers in Christ as their first bishop." If this is true, then he preceded the beloved St. Patrick, who became the patron saint of Ireland. Perhaps they are even the same person. The work of promoting Christianity was painfully slow but steady. It was fiendishly difficult to replace the old beliefs of magical power, the sanctity of kin, and the holiness of nature with the new dogma of the Vatican. The church chose, cleverly, to embrace certain aspects of Celtic mythology to woo the people with what they knew and loved. As part of this strategy, certain pagan festivals were incorporated into the Christian calendar; Samhain became All Saints; Beltane was transformed into Whitsun, and the goddess Brigit became St. Brigid, with her special day at Imbolc.

Almost imperceptibly, the extravagant Celtic mythology, the stories of heroic, brilliant, gifted warriors, stern, wise and sometimes dreadful druids, and the exploits of the fearsome Fianna, shifted into the mists of the Otherworld and retreated to the earthen mounds that marked the Underworld. Their stories were replaced by the tales of the Little People, the *Aes Sidhe*. Legends of leprechauns were born, as well as other fae such as fairies, pixies, piskies, goblins, elves, brownies, and knockers. An adapted folklore of little people emerged and quickly filtered into the literature of Ireland, Scotland, and the new world, notably in the work of William Butler Yeats.

"Faeries, come take me out of this dull world,
For I would ride with you upon the wind,
Run on the top of the dishevelled tide,
And dance upon the mountains like a flame."

—By William Butler Yeats, from *The Land of Heart's Desire*

In the early twentieth century, there was a worldwide resurgence of interest in spirituality that followed paths other than those practiced by organized religions—mostly based on a church hierarchy and a strict dogmatic code. In this milieu, modern Druidism and Wicca beliefs became very popular, and there are now several well-established and serious organizations that are based on Celtic mythology. You can read more about this at http://www.druidry.org/druid-way/what-druidry/brief-history-druidry/history-modern-druidism

The Irish are said to be more superstitious than other races. This is questionable, but they do have an array of interesting beliefs. Here is a sample regarding the days of the week:

Monday—Avoid marriage or taking a loan.

Tuesday—Good day to marry or start a journey.

Wednesday—Good day for writing but avoid new projects.

Thursday—Good day for a christening but a bad day to be moving house.

Friday—Really unlucky day as this is when Adam and Eve were banished from the Garden of Eden. Don't prune a fruit tree because it will not bear for three years in a row.

Saturday—Lucky day except for marriage: tying the knot on this day means you may not live out the year!

Sunday—A good day for a wedding. If you are unlucky enough to receive a knife wound on a Sunday, it will take a long time to heal.

Ireland has produced many outstanding artists and in particular fine writers, among them William Butler Yeats. I give the last words to him:

"The Celt, and his cromlechs, and his pillar-stones, these will not change much—indeed, it is doubtful if anybody at all changes at any time. In spite of hosts of deniers, and asserters, and wise-men, and professors, the majority still are adverse to sitting down to dine thirteen at a table, or being helped to salt, or walking under a ladder, of seeing a single magpie flirting his chequered tale. There are, of course, children of light who have set their faces against all this, although even a newspaperman, if you entice him into a cemetery at midnight, will believe in phantoms, for everyone is a visionary, if you scratch him deep enough. But the Celt, unlike any other, is a visionary without scratching."

—William Butler Yeats